Educational Adviser: Lynda Snowdon
Designer: Julian Holland
Picture researcher: Stella Martin
Artist for Contents pages: Penny Thomson

Photo credits:
J. Allan Cash, 4-5, 14-17; Biofotos, 18-19, 22-23;
Bruce Coleman, 6-9, 20-21, 24-25; England Scene, 30-31;
Stella Martin, 10-11; Natural History Photographic
Agency, 26-27; David Palmer, 28-29; ZEFA, 12-13
Cover picture: Bruce Coleman

Dillon Press, Inc., 242 Portland Avenue South
Minneapolis, Minnesota 55415

This edition published by Dillon Press by arrangement
with Macmillan Children's Books, London, England.
© Macmillan Publishers Limited, 1982

Library of Congress Cataloging-in-Publication Data

Naylor, Sue.
   The natural wonders of the world.

   (International picture library)
   Summary: Introduces some of the world's natural
wonders, including the Himalayas, Grand Canyon, and
Giant's Causeway.
   1. Landforms—Juvenile literature.   2. Natural monu-
ments—Juvenile literature.   [1. Landforms.   2. Natural
monuments]   I. Title.   II. Series.
GB401.5.N39   1986   910   86-2026
ISBN 0-87518-331-X

The Natural Wonders
of the World

Sue Naylor

DILLON PRESS, INC.
Minneapolis, Minnesota 55415

Contents

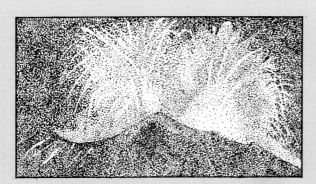

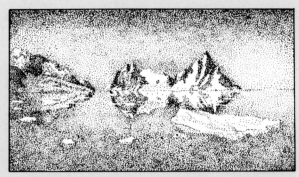

Volcano Erupting, Papua New Guinea
You could never stand this close to
an erupting volcano. It would be
boiling hot. There would be loud bangs

and rumbles from inside the earth.
Red-hot rock called lava would
spout out of the top and pour down
the side like a river of fire.

The Iguassu Falls, Brazil
The noise from these waterfalls is
tremendous. Large trees and bushes
can be carried over the edge by the

powerful river. The weather looks misty.
This is because of the spray from the
water as it hits the rocks. There is
a rainbow. How many colors can you see?

Desert in Spring, New Mexico
Few people, animals or plants can live
in a desert. It is usually too dry
and empty. But it has just rained here.

Millions of bright yellow flowers have opened. Look at the tall spiky plants. Their leaves are thin so they do not use much water.

Monument Valley, Arizona
There are no trees or rivers in this valley. The rocks have been shaped by the wind and the weather. What do

you think the weather is like here?
The valley is a long way from any
town, and tourists drive out to see
the rocks. You can see a car on the road.

11

Surfing, Hawaii

Crash! Imagine the roar as these huge
surf waves tumble down around you.
Some of them can be twice as high as

a person. The man in this photograph is
on a surfboard. He is using his arms to
help him balance. He could travel as
far as .6 mile (1 kilometer) across the surf.

The Midnight Sun, Norway
The sun is shining very strongly here
even though it is the middle of the
night. It is called the Midnight Sun.

Does the sun shine at night where you live? It only does this in places which are very far north or south, like Norway or Antarctica.

Cave Homes, Turkey

No, you are not on a strange planet!
These odd shapes were carved by
people hundreds of years ago. At that

time, people lived inside the caves
they had carved. Can you see doors,
windows and chimneys? No one lives here
now, but you can visit the caves.

17

Table Mountain, South Africa

The top of this mountain is flat,
just like the top of a table! Can you
see the fog that covers the top of the

mountain? This cloud is called the
"tablecloth." Look at the city, Capetown,
in front of the mountain. Even the large
buildings look small beside the mountain.

The Himalayas, Nepal
These mountains are the highest in
the world. They have very sharp, pointed
peaks. These are covered in snow all

year round. Can you see where the snow
begins? This is called the snow line.
The highest peak in the world is in the
Himalayas. It is called Mount Everest.

The Chocolate Hills, Philippines
There are more than one thousand of
these hills. They are all the same
shape and are covered in rough grass.

The grass turns the color of chocolate
in the summer when it is dry. In winter,
the hills are green. Palm trees grow
at the bottom of the hills.

Ayers Rock, Australia
This is the largest block of stone
in the world. It is in the desert in
Australia. Not many people live near

the rock. It is a different color at
different times of the day. What time
of the day do you think it is now?
Look at the color of the sky.

Antarctica

It is always freezing cold in Antarctica. Sometimes even the sea freezes. Today, the sea is like a mirror. You can see

reflections in the water. There is an
iceberg in the sea. You can only see
a small part of it because most of an
iceberg is under water.

The Grand Canyon, Arizona
This deep gorge was made by a river.
It took millions of years to be formed.
The river is now at the bottom of a

28

deep canyon. It would take you nearly
a whole day just to walk down there.
About 300 Havasupai Indians live near
the bottom of the canyon.

The Giant's Causeway, Northern Ireland
Most of these rocks have been shaped
into columns by nature. Each column
has six sides. A shape with six sides

is called a hexagon. Some of the columns
are taller than a person! The Giant's
Causeway was given its name because it
looks like a road made for giants.

31

Countries Featured in this Book

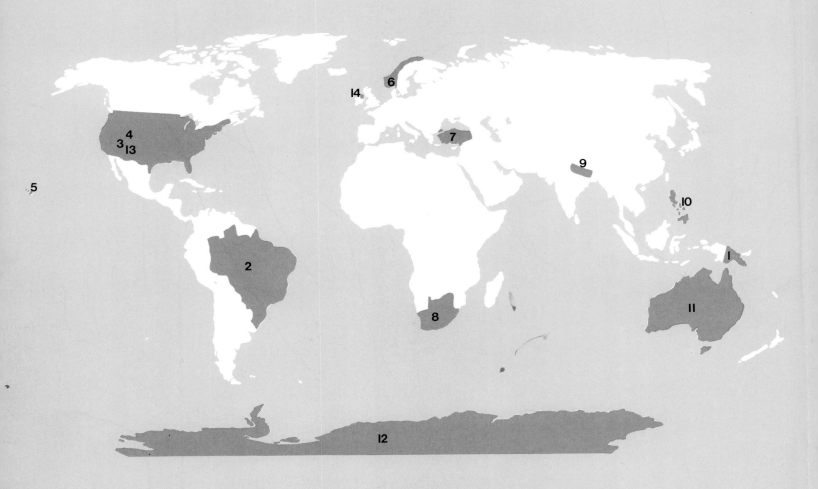